TABLE OF CONTENT

Introduction

Devices and technology have become an essential part of our day-to-day lives in the modern world. While these technological advancements have made our lives simpler and more convenient, they have likewise prompted the rise in device addictions that can be destructive to our mental health, social interactions, and overall well-being. This book "Digital Cleansing: Detox from Device Addictions" aims to help you overcome your device addiction and reclaim your life with practical strategies and advice.

In the present society, devices like cell phones, tablets, PCs, and different gadgets have turned into an indispensable part of our daily lives. We depend on them for communication, work, entertainment, and information. These devices have made our lives easier and more convenient, but they have also increased the number of people who are addicted to them, which can be bad for our physical, emotional, and mental health.

Device addiction refers to the compulsive and excessive use of devices, which can bring about ignoring other significant parts of life like social relationships, work, rest, and physical activity. The addictive nature of technology has been intentionally designed by tech companies to keep us hooked on their products and services. Subsequently, a considerable lot of us end up continually taking a look at our telephones, scrolling through social media, and engaging in other forms of screen time, even when we know it's not healthy for us

This book "Digital Cleansing: Detox from Device Addictions" aims to help you overcome your device addiction and reclaim your life with practical strategies and advice. It will guide you through the process of understanding the psychology of addiction and how technology can be addictive. It will likewise give you a 30-day plan to assist you with lessening your device usage gradually, mindfulness and meditation techniques to manage your device addiction and improve your overall mental health, and tips on how to create a healthy relationship with technology

In the end, the purpose of this book is to give you the tools you need to take charge of how you use your devices and live a life that is more balanced and satisfying. You can free yourself from device addiction and enjoy the benefits of being fully present and engaged in the world around you with the right mindset and tools.

Chapter 1

Understanding Device Addictions.

In this chapter, we'll look at the concept of Device Addictions and how it affects our lives. We will examine the psychological and behavioral factors that contribute to device addiction and how devices and technology have been designed to keep us hooked.

The widespread adoption of technology into our day-to-day lives has led to the development of device addiction which is a relatively new phenomenon. Addiction is a complex condition that involves the compulsive use of a substance or behavior despite negative consequences. Although there is no official diagnosis for device addiction, it is recognized as a growing problem that can harm mental health, social relationships, and overall well-being.

People do not get addicted to Technology and devices are not by accident. Tech organizations have planned their products and services to be Addictive. To keep us hooked and coming back for more, they employ a variety of strategies, including gamification, notifications, and social validation. As a result, even when there is no real reason to do so, we find ourselves obsessively checking our phones or other devices.

Notwithstanding the psychological and behavioral factors that add to device addiction, there are likewise physiological factors. Blue light from screens can disrupt sleep patterns, and devices' constant brain stimulation can cause anxiety, stress, and other mental health issues, according to studies.

The first step toward breaking free from device addiction is comprehending the factors that contribute to it. You can take steps to reduce your use and regain control of your life by becoming aware of the addictive nature of technology and devices. We'll look at practical ways to help you get over your device addiction and build a healthy relationship with technology in the following chapters.

Despite the potential negative effects of device addiction, it is essential to acknowledge the numerous advantages of technology and devices. They have reformed how we work, communicate, and access information. They can assist us in maintaining connections with loved ones, boosting our productivity, and providing us with entertainment and pleasure.

However, as with any tool or substance, moderation, and intention are essential when utilizing technology.

The Topics covered in this chapter shall include:
a. Definition and impact of device addiction
b. Psychological and behavioral factors that contribute to device addiction
c. The addictive nature of devices and technology
d. Physiological factors that contribute to device addiction
e. The importance of understanding device addiction in breaking free from it

By the end of this chapter, you should have a clear understanding of what device addiction is and how it can impact your life. This knowledge will be essential in taking the necessary steps to reduce your device usage and create a healthier relationship with technology.

Device addiction can affect our mental and emotional health in more ways than one. As we struggle to keep up with the constant demands and notifications from our devices, it can result in feelings of anxiety, and stress. Addiction to a device can also cause us to lose touch with the world around us because we become more focused on our screens than on the people and activities around us.

Moreover, gadget fixation can have negative consequences on our actual well-being. Excessive screen time can prompt eye strain, migraines, and neck and back pain. It can likewise disturb our sleep patterns, making it difficult to fall asleep and stay asleep.

Recognizing that device addiction is not just a personal issue is essential. It's also a social problem that affects how we get along with other people. We may miss out on important social and emotional connections that are essential to our well-being if we prioritize our devices over face-to-face interactions.

Understanding that it is not just a matter of willpower or self-control to break free from device addiction is essential. The purposeful addictive nature of technology and devices necessitates a methodical and deliberate approach to overcoming them.

You can use the strategies and tools in this book to overcome your device addiction and reclaim your life. You can improve your mental, emotional, and physical health as well as your overall well-being by developing a healthier relationship with technology and becoming more mindful of how you use devices.

One of the mental and social factors that add to gadget enslavement is the requirement for moment delight. We have instant access to information, entertainment, and social interaction thanks to technology and devices.

This can make a need to get moving and make it challenging for us to disengage from our gadgets.

Another factor is the fear of missing out (FOMO). Social media and other Applications constantly bombard us with notices, making a feeling of uneasiness and strain to stay connected and up-to-date.

The design of gadgets and technology also contributes to their addictive nature. To keep us hooked and coming back for more, app developers and tech companies employ a variety of strategies, such as gamification and notifications.

Addiction to a device can also have a physiological impact on our brain chemistry. Excessive screen time has been linked, according to research, to changes in the reward system in the brain, similar to what happens with substance addiction.

We can become more aware of our device usage patterns and how they may be contributing to addiction by comprehending these factors. By recognizing the underlying psychological, behavioral, and physiological factors, we can begin to take steps to break free from device addiction and create a healthier relationship with technology.

Our productivity may also suffer as a result of our device addiction because we may spend more time watching videos or social media than completing our responsibilities.

By understanding the effect of gadget dependence, we can start to do whatever it takes to break free from it. We should initially perceive the indications of habit and understand the factors that contribute to it.
In the following chapters, we'll look at practical ways to help you break free of device addiction and build a healthier relationship with technology. We'll give you tools to figure out how much you use your devices now and show you how to do it better.

By the end of this book, you will have the information and tools you need to take control of how you use your devices and build a better relationship with technology. While avoiding the negative effects of addiction, you can take advantage of the advantages of technology and devices.

Let's delve deeper into the psychological and behavioral factors that contribute to addiction now that we have established the significance of understanding device addiction.

The fact that technology and devices are made to be addictive is one of the primary reasons we have many people addicted to it. Notifications, rewards, and social pressure are just a few of the methods used by the app and game developers to create an addictive experience. These procedures trigger the release of dopamine in the brain, a neurotransmitter associated with pleasure and reward.

Particularly, social media platforms are made to keep users interested and scrolling for as long as possible. Content that is most likely to keep users engaged, despite not necessarily being informative or relevant, is given preference by algorithms.

Aside from the design of devices and technology, there also underlying psychological factors that contribute to addiction. Devices are used by many people to deal with stress, anxiety, and other negative emotions. Social media can likewise give a feeling of validation and acceptance, which can be addictive for certain individuals.

Behavioral factors, such as boredom and procrastination, can also lead to excessive device use. When we are bored or have a task that we do not want to complete, it is easy to turn to our devices for distraction.

To break free from device addiction, we can begin developing strategies by comprehending these psychological and behavioral factors. We'll go over a variety of methods in the following chapters to help you cut down on your device use and develop healthier tech habits.

Chapter 2

Identifying Your Device Addiction Triggers

To break free from device addiction, it is important to identify the triggers that lead you to use your devices excessively. Anything that makes you feel strongly or makes you want to reach for your device can act as a trigger, such as boredom, stress, anxiety, or the fear of missing out (FOMO).

You can reduce your reliance on devices by taking proactive measures to avoid or manage your triggers by identifying them. Here are some steps to assist you with identifying your device addiction triggers:

I.) Keep a device usage log: Begin by recording when and how frequently you use your devices throughout the day. Keep track of the time, the activity, and your feelings before and after using your device. You'll be able to identify patterns and potential triggers.

II.) Reflect on your emotions: Consider how you feel whenever you use your device too much. Are you feeling bored, stressed out, or anxious? Do you put off unpleasant tasks or use your device to distract yourself from negative feelings?

III.) Identify external triggers: Focus on outside factors that might set off your gadget utilization, for example, notifications, social media updates, or the presence of other people using their devices.

Consider your environment: Your environment can likewise assume a part in triggering device addiction. Do you tend to use your device more when you are in sure places, for example, at home or work? Are there certain times of day when you are bound to excessively utilize your gadget?

You can come up with a strategy for managing your device addiction more healthily by figuring out what triggers it. Setting limits on how much time you spend on devices, practicing mindfulness or other relaxation techniques to manage stress and anxiety, or finding new things to do when you're bored or restless are all examples of this.

We'll talk about practical ways to cut down on device use and build a better relationship with technology in the next chapter.

Chapter 3
Creating Healthy Habits

In this chapter, we will take a look at practical steps you can take to create healthy habits around your device use. We'll talk about the advantages of mindfulness, the power of routine, and how to limit your use of devices. We'll also talk about how important it is to find other things to do when you're not using your devices.

MINDFULNESS
Practicing mindfulness is one of the most effective strategies for overcoming a device addiction. Stress and anxiety, which are frequently the causes of device addiction, can be reduced by concentrating on the present moment.

Mindfulness is the practice of being intentionally aware and involved in the happenings around you. Mindfulness can be a powerful tool for breaking free from the demands and constant distractions of technology.

Practices of mindfulness can take many different forms. Meditation, in which you focus on your breath or a specific sensation, like the feeling of your feet on the ground, is a common practice. You simply acknowledge the thought and gently bring your attention back to the present moment when it unavoidably wanders. Stress can be reduced, focus and attention can be improved, and a sense of calm and relaxation can be fostered through this practice.

Exercising mindfulness through deep breathing is another method. Focusing on your breath as it enters and exits your body while taking slow, deep breaths is required for these exercises. Profound breathing can assist with diminishing pressure and uneasiness, lower circulatory strain, and advance sensations of unwinding.

By simply paying attention to your experiences and surroundings, mindfulness can also be practiced in everyday life. Pay attention to your body sensations, the sounds around you, and your feelings while you are using your phone or computer. You can resist the urge to mindlessly check your email or social media by becoming aware of your experiences.

Regular mindfulness practice can help you become more aware of how your addiction to devices is affecting your life. You can begin to develop healthier habits and achieve greater life balance by paying attention to your thoughts and feelings regarding your use of devices. Additionally, it may assist you in becoming more present and involved in your relationships as well as other activities, which may result in a greater sense of happiness and fulfillment.

The Power of Routine

Developing a routine for using your device can be a potent strategy for overcoming addiction. You can lessen the urge to check your phone or laptop regularly by scheduling specific times when you can use your device. This can likewise assist you with keeping on track and is useful, as you will know when the time has come to work and when the time has come to unwind.

Identifying the times of day when you need to be on your devices, such as for work or school, is the first step in creating a routine. Then, put away specific times for relaxation exercises, for example, checking social media or watching TV.

The power of routine cannot be overstated when it comes to breaking free from device addiction. Be sure to stick to it as closely as you can and include breaks for exercise and other activities. Establishing healthy boundaries around your use of devices and curbing your urge to constantly check your phone or computer can both be helped by developing a routine. It can be helpful to create a schedule or planner to help you stay on track.

It is essential to begin developing a routine by determining the times of day when you require access to electronic devices, such as for work or school. Set aside specific times for leisure activities like checking social media or watching television once you have identified these times. To help you stay on track, making a schedule or planner can be helpful.

It can be helpful to set reminders or alarms on your phone or computer to notify you when it's time to switch activities to keep your routine as consistent as possible. This can help you resist the urge to use your devices after your scheduled times.

Make sure to schedule breaks for activities like exercise. This can help you maintain your physical and mental health and lessen your need to check your phone or computer constantly. It can also assist you in remaining focused and productive during designated times when you use your device.

Keep in mind that developing a routine is a process, and figuring out what works best for you may require some trial and error. Be patient and kind to yourself as you work to lay out healthy habits around your device use. Your routine may become second nature to you over time, allowing you to live a life that is more balanced and satisfying.

Setting Boundaries

Setting Boundaries on how you use your devices is another important part of developing healthy device habits. This could mean turning off notifications at specific times of the day, limiting the amount of time you spend on social media, or completely avoiding devices while eating or participating in other social activities.

To define limits, begin by recognizing the particular manners by which your gadget use is affecting your life. The next step is to establish specific guidelines for when and how you will use your devices. Communicate these boundaries to your family, friends, and coworkers so that they can respect the time you spend without a device. Setting boundaries for your device use is essential for breaking free of addiction and developing healthy habits. It can assist you with being more present and participating in your routine, lessen pressure and uneasiness, and work on your associations with others.

To begin setting boundaries, determine the specific ways in which using your device is affecting your life. Do you end up continually looking at your device during dinners or get-togethers? Are you answering emails from work or scrolling through social media late at night? Set clear boundaries for yourself regarding when and how you will use your devices after you have identified these behaviors.

You could, for instance, decide to disable notifications at specific times of the day, such as when you eat meals or spend time with friends and family. You can also set a daily time limit for browsing social media to limit your time there. Establishing device-free areas, like your bedroom or during certain activities, may also be beneficial.

Communication of boundaries with others, including family, friends, and coworkers, is essential when establishing boundaries. They may appreciate your time without a device and come to appreciate your priorities as a result. You might also think about setting limits with other people, like not checking your work email after a certain time or not calling while you're eating dinner.

Keep in mind that setting boundaries is about finding a balance in your life and giving your priorities a priority. It might require an investment to lay out these propensities, yet over the long haul, you might find that defining limits becomes simpler and more normal. You can live a life that is more satisfying and well-balanced if you do this.

Finding Activities other than electronic Gadgets

Finally, to break free from device addiction, it is important to find alternative activities to replace the time you spend on your devices. Finding a new hobby, spending more time outside, or simply spending more time with friends and family are all examples of this.

Start by considering the activities you enjoy outside of using your device. Schedule time each day or week to participate in these activities by making a list. You can lessen your reliance on technology and create a more balanced life by engaging in activities that are fulfilling outside of your devices.

Finding alternative activities is an essential component of breaking free from device addiction and creating a more satisfying life. You can lessen your reliance on technology and achieve a better balance in your life by engaging in activities that you enjoy and that make you feel happy and fulfilled.

Start by considering the activities you enjoy outside of using your device to find alternative activities. Reading, working out, cooking, gardening, and spending time with friends and family are all examples of this. Make a rundown of these exercises and put away opportunities every day or week to participate in them.

It can likewise be useful to attempt new exercises and side interests. If you want to learn something new and meet new people, think about taking a class or joining a club. This can assist you with tracking down new interests and interests beyond your gadgets.

Spending time outdoors can likewise be an extraordinary method for detaching from your gadgets and partaking in your general surroundings. Go for a climb, take a bicycle ride, or just go for a stroll in nature. It has been proven that spending time in nature improves overall well-being and reduces stress and anxiety.

Keep in mind, finding elective exercises is tied in with making balance in your life and finding exercises that give you pleasure and satisfaction. It might require some time to find the exercises that turn out best for you, however by investigating new side interests and investing energy outside, you can lessen your reliance on gadgets and make a more adjusted and satisfying life.

In conclusion, device addiction is a growing problem in today's world, and it can have negative impacts on our mental and physical health, relationships, and overall well-being. However, by taking intentional steps to break free from addiction and establish healthy device habits, we can reclaim control of our lives and live more fulfilling, balanced lives.

Practicing mindfulness, setting routines and boundaries, and finding alternative activities are all key components of creating healthy device habits. By being present at the moment, setting clear rules for ourselves, and engaging in fulfilling activities outside of our devices, we can reduce our dependence on technology and create a more balanced life.

Breaking free from device addiction is a process that requires commitment, patience, and effort. However, the benefits outweigh the effort. By taking control of our device use, we can reduce stress and anxiety, improve our relationships, and live happier, healthier lives. So, take the first step today and start creating healthy habits around your device use.

Chapter 4

Digital Detox

Sometimes, going cold turkey is the best way to get rid of your device addiction. We'll look at the idea of a digital detox and how to put it into practice in this chapter. We will show you how to get ready for a digital detox, what to expect during the process, and how to keep your digital detox going for a long time.

Introduction to Digital detox

Digital detox is a time when you deliberately disconnect from technology and devices. It tends to be a strong method for resetting your relationship with technology and breaking free from device addiction.

It's easy to believe that we can't live without our gadgets in today's world. We, on the other hand, can. And sometimes, disconnecting from technology can help us connect with the world around us and live more fully in the now.

Preparing for a Digital Detox

Before beginning a digital detox, it's important to set yourself up for success. Here are some suggestions to help you with planning:

a. Set a goal: Find out why you want to do a digital detox and what you want to get out of it. Throughout the process, this will assist you in remaining focused and motivated.

b. Inform others: Let friends, family, and coworkers know that you will disconnect from technology for a while. Expectations will be better managed and there will be less pressure to answer calls or messages as a result.

c. Plan alternative activities: Choose alternative activities that you can do during your digital detox. Hobbies, outdoor activities, social gatherings, or simply spending time with loved ones are all examples of this.

d. Prepare for discomfort: If you're used to being connected constantly, it's normal to feel uneasy when you disconnect from technology. Find healthy ways to deal with withdrawal symptoms, like exercise or meditation, and be prepared to experience some of them.

You will deliberately disconnect from technology during a digital detox. This can be an extremely challenging but also extremely rewarding experience.

What to Expect During a Digital Detox

i. Feelings of boredom: We might initially feel bored if we don't have the technology to distract us. Embrace this feeling and use it as a chance to investigate new exercises or side interests.

ii. Increased presence: We may find that we are more aware of our surroundings and present at the moment when technology is not present.

iii. Improved sleep: Our sleeping patterns may be disrupted by excessive device use. You might notice that you get a better night's sleep and feel more rested when you do a digital detox.

vi. Increased productivity: We might be able to concentrate better and be more productive if we don't have to deal with notifications and messages all the time.

After completing a digital detox, it is essential to maintain healthy device habits over the long term. Here are some suggestions to get you started:

1. Set boundaries: Set clear guidelines for when and how you will use your gadgets. This could be as simple as turning off notifications at specific times of the day, limiting your time spent on social media, or completely avoiding devices during meals or other social events.

2. Practice mindfulness: Be present and aware of how you use your device. Before reaching for your phone, take a moment to ponder and observe when you are tempted to do so.

3. Find alternative activities: Make time for fulfilling activities that you enjoy outside of technology regularly.

4. Be kind to yourself: It takes time to overcome a device addiction, so it's important to be patient with yourself and kind to yourself along the way.

Conclusion

Resetting your relationship with technology and breaking free from device addiction can be accomplished effectively through a digital detox. You can lead a life that is happier, healthier, and more balanced if you prepare for the procedure, know what to expect, and stick to healthy device habits over time.

Chapter 5:
Managing Device Use in the Workplace

Many jobs today require us to be connected to our devices. In any case, this can add to devise addiction and adversely influence our efficiency and mental health.

Setting Boundaries

One way to manage device use in the workplace is to set boundaries around when and how you use your devices. In this chapter, we'll show you how to do that, as well as how to communicate with your employer and find other ways to stay focused. For instance, you can switch off notifications during specific times of the day or limit your time on social media during work hours. To avoid being distracted throughout the day, you can also schedule specific times to check your messages or email.

Communicating with Your Employer

It's also critical to keep in touch with your employer about any issues you may be having with your device use. You can discuss how your productivity and well-being are impacted by excessive device use and seek assistance managing it. You might be able to get help staying focused and productive from your employer in the form of tools for managing your time or counseling services.

Finding Alternative Ways to Stay Focused

Lastly, finding other ways to stay focused can be a useful tool for controlling employee device use at work. This could mean taking frequent breaks to stretch or walk around the office, setting a timer to keep your attention on the task at hand for a predetermined amount of time, or listening to music or white noise to block out other distractions.

You can manage device use in the workplace and maintain a healthy work-life balance by communicating with your employer, establishing boundaries, and finding alternative means of staying focused. Keep in mind that putting your well-being and productivity first is crucial, and managing your device use in a way that suits you best often requires conscious effort.

Nowadays, many jobs require us to be connected to our devices constantly, but this constant connection can lead to devise addiction, reduce productivity, and affect our mental health. To oversee gadget use in the working environment, it's critical to define limits, speak with your manager, and track down alternative ways of remaining on track.

Instead of checking email and messages constantly throughout the day, one effective strategy is to schedule specific times to check them. You'll be able to focus on your work better and avoid being constantly distracted by this. It's also important to avoid multitasking because it can make you more stressed and less productive. Instead, give each task your full attention and concentrate on it one at a time.

Managing employee device use can also be made easier with the help of productivity tools. Time-management apps, project-management software, and distraction-blocking apps can all help you stay organized and focused. You might also find that taking regular breaks throughout the day helps you refuel and remain focused. Try taking a short walk, doing some stretching exercises, or simply closing your eyes and taking a few deep breaths.

You can also stay motivated and focused by setting goals for your workday that are attainable. Break your assignments into more modest, reachable objectives and focus on them because of their significance and earnestness. Additionally, don't be afraid to discuss your device usage and productivity requirements with your employer. You can control your workplace device use and maintain a healthy work-life balance by figuring out what works best for you and being deliberate about how you use your devices.

Furthermore, defining limits with your gadgets in the workplace is significant. This might mean switching off notifications during specific times of the day, for example, during gatherings or when you want to zero in on an undertaking. You can likewise set explicit times during the day for browsing messages instead of continually looking at them over the course of the day.

Communicating with your employer about your device use and any concerns is also helpful. Talk to your supervisor or a representative from human resources about possible solutions if you believe that your use of devices is harming your mental health or productivity.

Lastly, it can be helpful to find alternative strategies for staying focused at work. Utilizing time management strategies like the Pomodoro method or apps or tools to block distracting websites or apps during work hours are examples of this. Other options include taking breaks to stretch or walk around.

You can achieve a better work-life balance, reduce stress, and increase productivity at work by controlling your device use. Keep in mind that achieving the ideal balance will require some time and effort, but the rewards will be well worth it.

The Pomodoro Technique explained
The Pomodoro technique is a time management strategy that can be useful for controlling device use and increasing workplace productivity. It includes separating

work into centered spans, commonly 25 minutes in length, trailed by brief breaks.

To utilize the Pomodoro strategy, start by choosing a task that needs to be completed. Work on the task until the timer goes off, then set a timer for 25 minutes. Then, take a brief break, usually between five and ten minutes. Rehash this cycle multiple times, and afterward have some time off of 15-20 minutes.

Because it encourages you to focus on a single task at a time and to take frequent breaks, the Pomodoro method can be useful for managing device use. This can help you stay on track with your work and reduce the temptation to constantly check your devices.

It is simple to incorporate the Pomodoro technique into your daily routine because there are numerous Pomodoro apps and timers available that can assist you in tracking your work intervals and breaks.

Chapter 6:

Device Addiction in Children

Addiction to devices isn't just a problem for adults. Children are also at risk of developing an addiction to electronic devices, which can have serious effects on their growth and health. In this section, we will investigate how to perceive device addiction in children and give tips on how to create healthy device habits for them.

Signs of Device Addiction in Children

It very well may be hard to recognize device addiction in kids, particularly when gadgets are progressively being utilized for educational purposes. In any case, there are a few signs to pay special attention to, for example,

1. Mood swings or irritability when device use is limited

2. Lack of interest in non-device-related activities

3. Physical symptoms such as eye strain or headaches

4. Creating Healthy Device Habits for Children.

It is important to establish clear boundaries and guidelines regarding device use to create healthy device habits for children. Here are a few hints:

Limit screen time: Maintain a daily time limit for children's use of electronic devices.

Encourage alternative activities: Playing outside, reading, and drawing are just a few of the things kids can do without using a device.

Set device-free zones: Make certain rooms in the house, like the dining room table and the bedroom, device-free zones.

Model healthy device habits: Children learn by example, so it's important to lead by example and use devices safely.

Monitor device usage: Be aware of your child's app and website usage and monitor their device usage.

Keep in mind that overcoming a device addiction is a process, and it may take some time for children to adjust to their new routines. Be patient, be consistent, and explain to your child why developing healthy device habits is important. You can help prepare your child for a lifetime of healthy device use by doing so.

Excessive device use, difficulty with offline activities, irritability or restlessness when devices are taken away, and a decline in academic or social performance which are some of the symptoms of device addiction in children can be history if healthy device habits are formed.

From a young age, it is essential to establish clear rules and boundaries regarding device use to aid in the prevention of device addiction in children. This might include restricting screen time, setting device-free zones in the home, and empowering and encouraging offline activities like outside play and imaginative leisure activities.

By setting an example of responsible device use, parents and other caregivers can also help children develop healthy device habits. This includes not using devices excessively in front of children, giving offline activities a priority, and not using devices during meals or family time.

Parents must also communicate openly and honestly with their children about the dangers of device addiction and the need to strike a healthy balance between using devices and other activities.

It may be necessary to seek professional assistance if a child already suffers from device addiction. To address the underlying issues that contribute to addiction and to develop healthy coping strategies and habits, this may include therapy or counseling.

In conclusion, a proactive approach and a commitment to establishing a healthy balance between device use and other activities are necessary to prevent children from becoming addicted to devices. By defining clear principles and limits, modeling healthy device habits, and seeking professionals when important, we can assist our youngsters with creating sound healthy habits around device use and setting them up for a happy and fulfilling life.

CHAPTER 7
SUMMARY

Although it is challenging, breaking free of a device addiction is doable. You can take control of your device use and live a healthier, more fulfilling life by understanding the psychology of device addiction, developing healthy habits, implementing a digital detox, managing device use in the workplace, and recognizing the risks for children.

Keep in mind that device addiction is a growing problem that may require some time and effort to overcome. However, the effort is well worth it if you want to reduce device use and improve your relationship with technology. Overcoming device addiction and creating a life that is more balanced and fulfilling can be accomplished with persistence, patience, and self-compassion.

Keep in mind that breaking free of a device addiction is a process, and finding the right balance might take some time. If you need help, don't be afraid to ask friends, family, or a professional for help. With effort and commitment, you can decrease your reliance on devices and create a more balanced life.

Last but not least, it's essential to keep in mind that technology isn't necessarily bad. It has the potential to offer numerous advantages and enhance our lives in numerous ways. Notwithstanding, it ultimately depends on us to utilize it mindfully and with some restraint. We can harness the power of technology without succumbing to its addictive qualities by paying attention to how we use our devices and placing our health above all else.

Thank you for reading this guide on device addiction. We sincerely hope that it has aided you in developing a more positive relationship with technology.